SOUND AND MUSIC

Barbara Taylor

Photographs by Peter Millard

FRANKLIN WATTS
New York • London • Toronto • Sydney

Franklin Watts, Inc
387 Park Avenue South
New York, NY 10016

Design: Janet Watson

Science consultant: Dr. Bryson Gore

Primary science adviser: Lillian Wright

Series editor: Debbie Fox

Editor: Roslin Mair

Illustrations: Linda Costello

The author and publisher would like to thank the following children for their participation in the photography of this book: Joanna Archer, Shola Austin, Sam Bartlett, Colleen Delaney, Karim Dlimi, Charmaine Gentle, Bonita KC, Roshan Meghani, Nishma Patel, Kedisha Raman, Paul Stocker, Kirstie Wallace, Peter Willan.

Thanks to Carol Olivier of Kenmont Primary School, Ganga Budhathoki and Mrs. Willan.

Library of Congress Cataloging-in-Publication Data
Taylor, Barbara, 1954-
Sound and music / Barbara Taylor.
p. cm. – (Science starters)
Includes index.
Summary: Suggests activities demonstrating how variations in the creation of sound can create musical tones for the human ear and why musical instruments produce sound.
ISBN 0-531-14185-3
1. Sound – Juvenile literature. 2. Sound-waves – Juvenile literature. 3. Music – Acoustics and physics – Juvenile literature. 4. Musical instruments – Juvenile literature. [1. Sound – Experiments. 2. Music – Experiments. 3. Experiments.] I. Title. II. Series.
QC225.5.T98 1991
534 – dc20 91-8740
CIP
AC

Printed in Belgium

CONTENTS

This book is all about how sounds are produced, the sounds made by musical instruments and how we hear sounds. It is divided into five sections. Each has a different colored triangle at the corner of the page. Use these triangles to help you find the different sections.

These red triangles at the corner of the tinted panels show you where a step-by-step investigation starts.

SOUND MESSAGES

What is your favorite kind of music?

Musical sounds change the way we feel about things. They can make us happy or sad, calm or angry, frightened or relaxed. In plays or movies, music is used to give the audience information about the emotions of the characters and change the mood of the performance. The rhythm or beat of instruments such as drums can also be used to send messages, or help people keep in step.

The everyday sounds around us give us all kinds of information. The ringing of an alarm clock helps us to get up on time. When the telephone or the doorbell rings, we know someone wants to speak to us. By talking to other people we find out what they are thinking and learn new ideas and ways of doing things. Groans or cries tell us that people are in pain or trouble and need our help.

In some sports, the referee blows a whistle to give the players information about the time or the rules of the game.

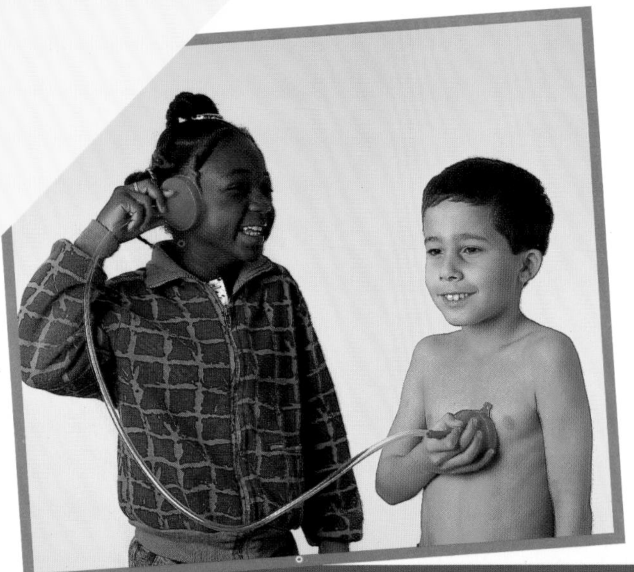

Doctors may use a stethoscope to listen to the sounds made by a person's heart or lungs. This helps them to tell if the person is ill and determine how to make them better. You can make your own stethoscope from a piece of plastic tubing with a funnel at each end. Use your stethoscope to listen to a friend's heartbeat.

Very loud sounds, such as bicycle horns or the sirens on police cars or fire engines, can be frightening. But they are also useful because they warn us of danger and tell people and vehicles to keep out of the way.

Two-way radios help rescue experts, such as fire fighters, to organize help and to rescue people quickly. They are especially useful in situations where the rescuers cannot see each other because of thick smoke or bad weather on roads, such as on the mountains.

MAKING SOUNDS

If you shake a "slinky" up and down on a tabletop, it squeezes together and stretches out again in a regular pattern. This is what happens to the air when sounds are made. The sounds squeeze, or press, together a package of air and when this expands, or stretches out again, it squeezes the air next to it. This happens over and over again, producing a whole series of squeezes and stretches as the sound is passed through the air.

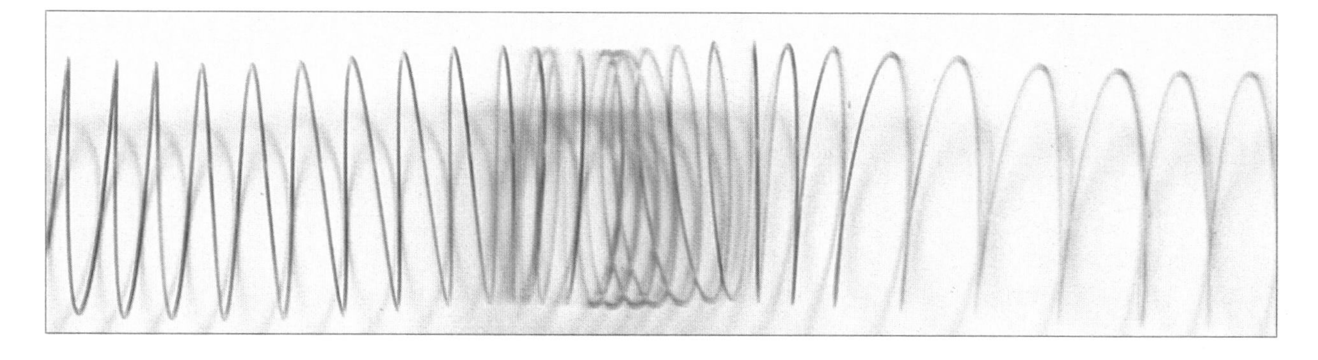

Because sounds have a regular pattern or frequency, like the waves on the sea, they are called sound "waves." But sounds are really very small changes in the pressure of the air.

We cannot see sounds, but we can hear them when our ears pick up the changes in air pressure (see pages 22-25.) When you clap, you squeeze air between your hands and the changes in air pressure make the sounds you hear.

Out in space, there is no air to be squeezed, so there are no sounds. Astronauts have to use radios to communicate with other astronauts outside the spacecraft. Radio waves are a type of electromagnetic radiation (a form of light energy), so they can travel through space like the Sun's rays.

Inside a spacecraft there is air, so the astronauts can talk to each other normally.

Rest your thumb and finger against your throat and say something. Can you feel the vibrations? When you speak, air is pushed from your lungs over flaps of elastic tissue, called vocal cords, in the throat.

To find out how your vocal chords work, blow up a balloon and stretch the neck sideways as you let the air out of the balloon. As you stretch the neck in and out, the sound will change.

In singing, changing the size of the opening between your vocal chords helps make different notes.

SOUNDS ON THE MOVE

If you watch someone making a loud noise, such as banging cymbals, from a distance, you will see them make the noise before you hear the sound. This is because sound travels much more slowly than light. In air, sound travels at about 1,083 feet a second. This is about a million times slower than the speed of light.

Sound travels at different speeds through materials. It travels faster through solids (such as wood or steel) than it does through air. This is because molecules that make up solids and liquids are closer together than in air. So they pass the changes in pressure through them more quickly.

Tape a watch on one side of a door and stand close to the door. Can you hear the watch ticking? Then press your ear right against the wood. Does this make a difference?

Have you ever noticed that the siren of a police car seems to drop to a lower note as it passes you? You can produce a similar effect by asking an adult to drill a hole in the end of a ruler and swinging it around and around above your head. How does the sound change as the ruler moves nearer to you and further away again?

This is called the Doppler effect, after the scientist who investigated it. It happens because sound waves from something coming towards you are squeezed together and make a high sound. Sound waves from something that is moving away from you are stretched out; they make a lower sound.

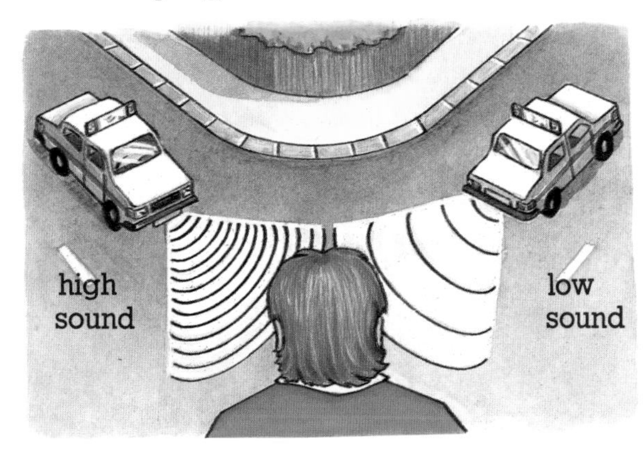

BOUNCING BACK

Try dropping marbles onto a hard surface and a soft surface. How is the sound different? When sound hits a surface, it bounces back, or is reflected. If the surface is far away from the object making the sound, you may hear the sound again a few seconds later as an echo. Soft surfaces soak up, or absorb, sounds so they do not bounce back as much. This makes sounds quieter.

In a concert hall, the shape of the hall and the materials it is made from control the way the music bounces off the walls and ceilings. Concert halls have to be carefully designed to cut down on unwanted echoes and make it possible for the audience to hear the music properly. The study of how the quality of sound is affected by the shape of a room and the materials it is made from is called acoustics.

Bats make high, squeaking sounds and use their large, sensitive ears to collect the echoes from objects around them. This is called echolocation and helps bats to find their way around in the dark and detect food, such as insects. The echo-squeaks made by bats are usually too high for us to hear.

Arrange two umbrellas in a straight line and whisper into the middle of one umbrella. A friend should hear what you are saying by putting their ear to the same point on the other umbrella. The curved dish shape of the umbrella focuses the sound of your voice at one point and reflects it to the other umbrella in a straight line. This helps to stop too much sound from being lost along the way and makes it louder.

NEW ERA
A
G
F
E
D
C

MUSIC

How many musical instruments can you think of? Musical instruments are designed to produce a series of different notes by plucking strings, blowing into or across pipes or hitting surfaces. They all have something which vibrates to squeeze the air and make musical sounds.

Percussion instruments
These produce sounds when you strike, shake or scrape them. They include drums, tablas, tambourines, cabassas, guiros, xylophones, maracas.

Stringed instruments
These produce sounds when they are played with a bow or the strings are plucked or hit with hammers. They include violins, cellos, guitars, sitars, harps, pianos and harpsichords.

Instruments with pipes
These produce sounds when you blow into or across the pipe. Woodwind instruments have holes in the pipe while brass instruments usually have a pipe that can change its length. They include recorders, flutes, clarinets, saxophones, trumpets and trombones.

STRINGS

In a stringed instrument, the note depends on how thick the string is, how long it is and how tightly it is stretched. Stretch a rubber band around a book and push two pencils under the band. With the pencils a long way apart, pluck the band with your finger. Then move the pencils closer together. Is the note you make higher or lower this time? Try plucking the string with your fingernail instead of your finger. This will give you a higher, sharper note.

In many stringed instruments, such as a guitar, the strings are stretched across a hollow box called a sound box. When the strings are plucked, they vibrate producing air waves to make the notes. But the vibrating strings also make the sound box vibrate. This squeezes up the air even more, producing a louder sound.

To find out more about the notes produced by strings, try this investigation:

1 Attach a long piece of tightly wound string to one end of a wooden board.

2 Tie weights, such as a bag of marbles, to the other end of the string.

3 Push two pencils under the string to lift it clear of the wood.

4 Start off with a small weight and pluck the string with your finger. Then gradually add more weights to stretch the string even further. As the string is stretched tighter, it makes a higher note. How many different notes can you make?

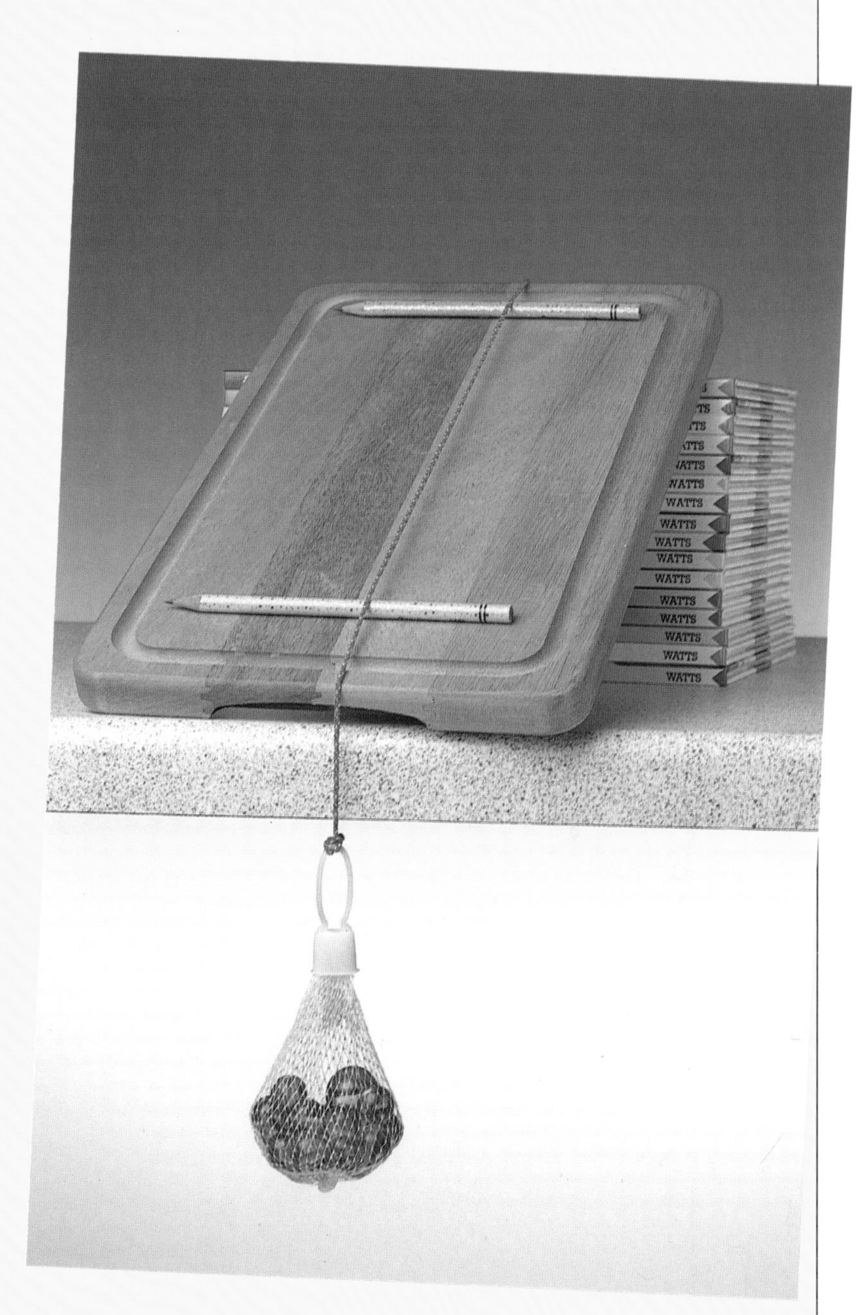

On a stringed instrument, the pegs at the end of the fingerboard can be turned to keep the strings stretched by the right amount to produce the different notes.

PIPES

In instruments with pipes, the note depends on the length of the column of air inside the pipe. The notes are caused by changes in air pressure as the air moves up and down the pipe. Some instruments, such as pan pipes, have a separate length of pipe for each note. Try cutting straws into different lengths and blowing across the top. Do the shorter pipes make higher or lower notes than the longer ones?

Other instruments, such as recorders, have only one pipe. You change the note by moving your fingers on and off the holes to change the length of the air column in the pipe. When a hole is open near the top of the recorder, air escapes through the hole and creates a short column of air.

Try making a bottle organ.

1 Collect several clean glass bottles which are the same size and shape.

2 Arrange the bottles in a line and fill them with different amounts of water.

3 Blow across the tops of the bottles. Each one gives out a different note. With a lot of air in the bottle, it vibrates slowly and produces a low note. With less air in the bottle, it vibrates quickly and produces a high note. Adjust the water levels in the bottles until you can produce a series of high and low notes.

4 Try tapping the bottles instead of blowing across them. How are the notes different?

PERCUSSION

Most percussion instruments produce noises rather than definite notes. You can make shakers from empty plastic cups, plastic bottles or old margarine tubs. Collect different fillings for your containers, such as rice, beans, pasta or buttons. Tape a lid on each container or tape two containers together to seal the fillings inside. Which fillings make the best sounds?

Kettledrums or tympani are the only drums in an orchestra that make definite notes. They have screws on the side which can be turned to tighten or loosen the skin and change the notes.

A drum consists of a skin stretched tightly over a hollow container. When you hit a drum, you make the skin vibrate and squeeze the air around it. The air inside the drum vibrates too, which makes the sound louder.

Try stretching some plastic wrap over a bowl. Tape down the edges and hit the plastic with a stick. If the plastic is tight, the skin will vibrate fast and produce a high note. What happens if the plastic is looser?

Try making several different drums to see how the shape and size of the containers, and the materials the drumskin is made of, change the sounds they make.

HEARING SOUNDS

We detect changes in the pressure of the air – sounds – with our ears. The outer part of the ear, on the side of your head, acts like a funnel to collect the sounds around us. The main part of the ear is inside the head. In this hidden, inner part, sounds are converted into electrical signals called nerve impulses, which carry the sound to the brain. The brain interprets the signals and tells us what we have heard.

How far away can you hear a pin drop? Ask a friend to drop a pin onto a metal tray. Keep moving further away until you can no longer hear the sound. You could make a chart of your results and compare them with your friends.

Most people can hear sounds which make the air vibrate at between 20 and 17,000 times a second. But some animals can hear higher or lower sounds than we can. This fennec fox has very sensitive hearing. Its huge ears collect the tiny sounds made by small animals and help it to hunt at night.

Having an ear on each side of the head helps us to tell which direction a sound is coming from. Ask a friend to sit with their back to you and make a sound such as jingling a bunch of keys. Can your friend point accurately to the source of the sound? Try the same test with one ear covered. Is it harder this time?

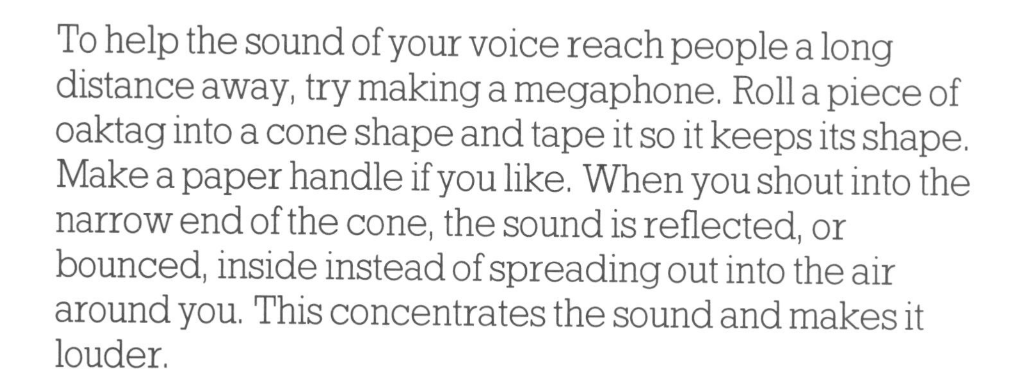

To help the sound of your voice reach people a long distance away, try making a megaphone. Roll a piece of oaktag into a cone shape and tape it so it keeps its shape. Make a paper handle if you like. When you shout into the narrow end of the cone, the sound is reflected, or bounced, inside instead of spreading out into the air around you. This concentrates the sound and makes it louder.

If you hold the narrow end of the megaphone against your ear, you can use it as an ear trumpet to help you hear more easily.

This frog uses its own throat to make its voice louder. It pushes air against the floor of its mouth, which expands like a balloon to make a sound box (see page 16).

The air inside the sound box vibrates to make the frog's calls louder.

Can you imagine a world without sound? About one child in a thousand is born profoundly deaf, and many people develop hearing problems later in life as a result of accidents or diseases such as measles and mumps. It is important to detect hearing problems as soon as possible so that treatment and help can be given. With care and encouragement from others, deafness need not prevent someone from leading a normal life. Many deaf people learn to play musical instruments.

Hearing aids pick up sounds and make them louder. A child may wear a radio receiver to pick up radio waves from a transmitter worn by a teacher. Radio waves do not lose as much strength as sound waves as they travel through the air.

Fingerspelling, sign language and lipreading (speech reading) also help deaf people to communicate. By using a mixture of signing systems, a deaf person can choose which way to express his or her ideas and feelings.

NOISE POLLUTION

Noise pollution consists of sounds that we find unpleasant or don't want. They may be produced by loud music, big trucks, airplanes or machines. Noise makes it hard for people to sleep and can lead to stress and illness. Very loud noises can damage our hearing.

People who work in noisy places should wear earplugs or earmuffs to protect their ears. Can you design some earmuffs to cut out unwanted noise? What materials might you choose?

The amount of noise in the environment can be cut down in other ways. Motorcycles, cars and trucks are fitted with mufflers to make their engines quieter. A car without a muffler sounds more like a tank. In buildings, double-glazed windows and carpets and curtains reduce the level of noise.

See if you can find out which materials are best at reducing the noise of a ticking clock. Try to silence the ticking by packing materials such as paper, plastic, cloth or yarn around the clock. Soft materials absorb some of the noise and keep it from escaping. Do the materials keep out more sound if they are packed tightly or loosely?

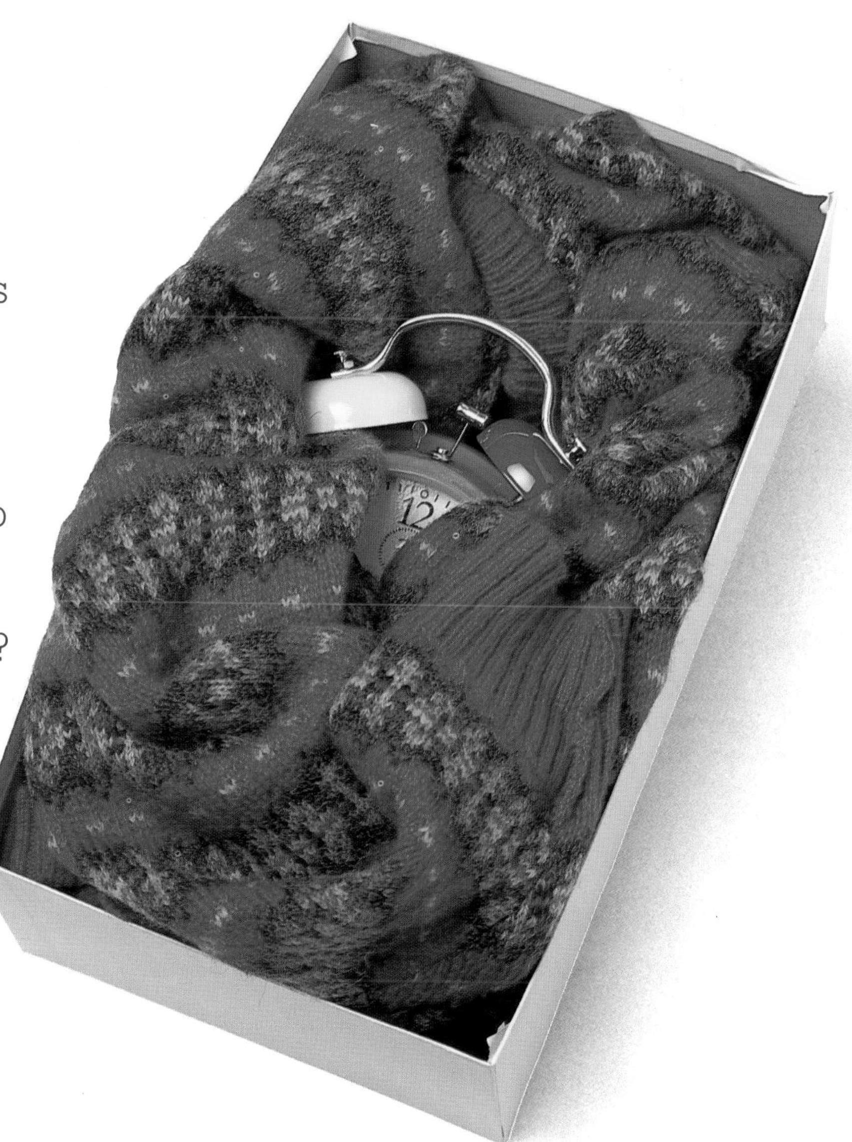

MORE THINGS TO DO

Yogurt cup telephone

Make a small hole in the bottom of two empty, clean yogurt cups. Cut a very long piece of tightly wound string and push one end through the bottom of each cup. Tie a knot inside each cup to keep the string from pulling out of the holes. Ask a friend to hold one of the cups to their ear. Move away from your friend until the string is straight and taut. Then speak quietly into the other cup. Can your friend hear what you are saying?

The vibrations of your voice make your cup vibrate and this in turn makes the string vibrate. The vibrations travel along the string to the other cup and pass into your friend's ear. Can you attach a third cup to make a three-way telephone?

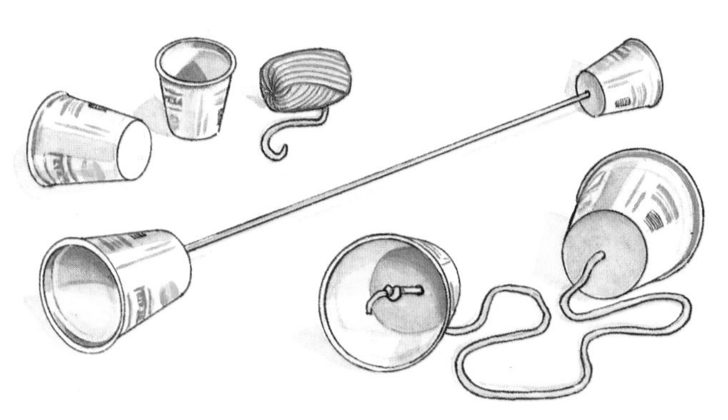

Making scrapers

Gather together objects with a rough surface or ridges along the sides. Here are some ideas: plastic bottles with ridges, corrugated paper, wicker baskets and egg cartons. You could also cover small pieces of wood with sandpaper. Play your scrapers by rubbing them against each other or use things like paintbrushes, scrubbing brushes, chopsticks or knitting needles to make scraping sounds. How many different sounds can you make?

Make a paper snapper

1 Cut out a piece of paper 5 inches square (5×5in). Draw two lines, each ¾ inch from the side of the paper.

2 Cut across the paper diagonally, keeping both the lines on one side of the scissors.

3 Cut out a piece of cardboard 8 inches square, and place it on the paper up against the two lines.

4 Fold the paper over the cardboard and tape it in place.

5 Turn the cardboard over and fold it in half diagonally so most of the paper is inside.

6 Grip the point of the cardboard away from the paper and flick it sharply through the air to make the paper snap out of the cardboard. This squeezes the air together with a lot of force, which you hear as a loud bang.

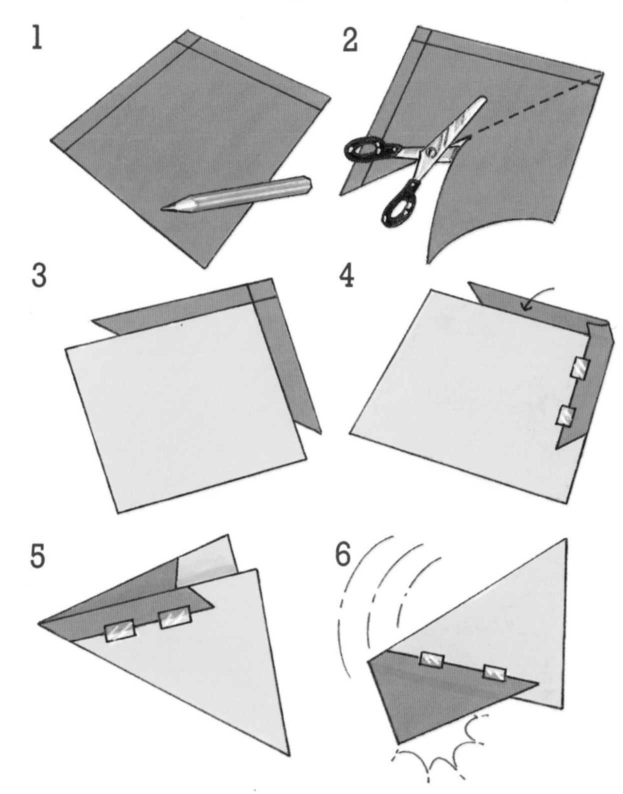

Sound tubes

Find two long cardboard tubes and place them at an angle on a table with the ends of the tubes about 2 inches apart. Place a piece of cardboard in an upright position about 2 inches away from the close ends of the tubes. Put something that makes a loud sound, such as an alarm clock, at the end of one tube and listen at the end of the other tube. You should still be able to hear the sound, even though the tubes are not joined together. The sound travels along one tube, bounces off the cardboard and is reflected into the other tube. If this doesn't work at first, adjust the angle of the tubes until you can hear the sound.

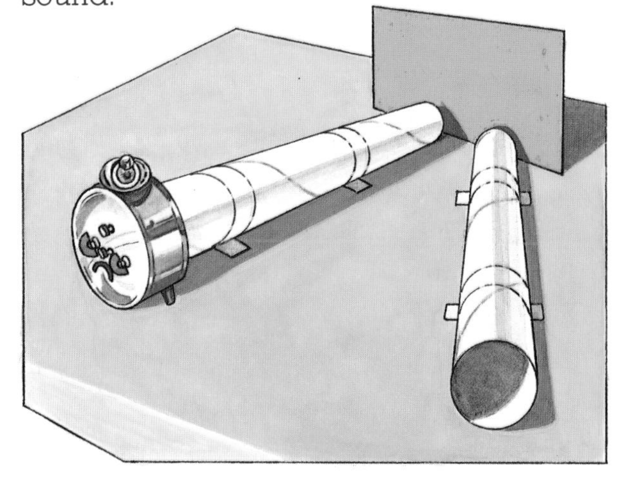

Guess the sound

Collect a variety of objects made from different materials, such as plastic, cellophane, cloth, cardboard, sponge, sandpaper, aluminum foil and glass. Use a large piece of cardboard or cloth to make a screen and ask your friends to sit on one side of the screen. Then make sounds with the objects in your collection. Can your friends guess the name of the object you are using to make the sound? Do they know what kind of material it is made from? How many different sounds can you make with one object?

Twanging a ruler

Hold a ruler so half of it is over the edge of a table. Twang it to make it vibrate up and down. What sound does it make? Move the ruler so only a short length hangs over the edge. A shorter length of ruler vibrates faster and makes a higher sound. What happens to the sound if a longer length of ruler is over the edge of the table?

Make a rubber band instrument

Find a thick piece of wood, some rubber bands (all the same size), some short nails and a hammer. Ask an adult to help you hammer the nails into the wood to match the picture. Stretch a rubber band between each pair of nails so some bands are stretched a lot and other bands are not stretched much at all. Pluck the rubber bands with your fingers. Which bands make high sounds? Which bands make low sounds? Now use rubber bands of different thicknesses.

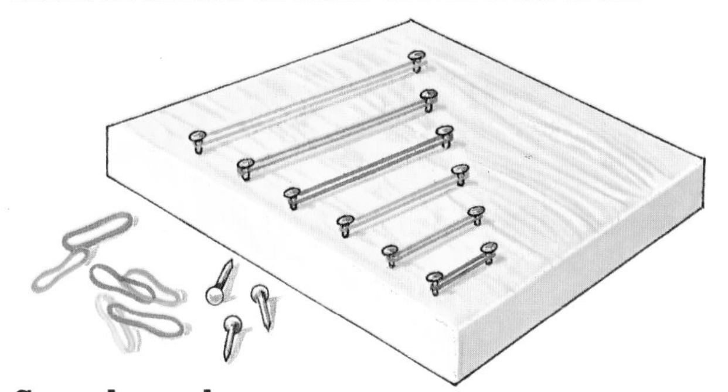

Sound words

See how many words you can think of which describe sounds. Some sound words, such as buzz, pop or hiss, try to copy the sounds themselves. These words are called onomatopoeic. Go on a walk outdoors and invent words to describe what you hear. When you have a good collection of words, sort them into groups, such as nice and nasty sounds. Use your sound words to write a story or a poem.

DID YOU KNOW?

▲ Women have higher voices than men because their vocal cords are usually shorter and more tightly stretched.

▲ Sound travels through water at about 4,692 feet per second – about five times faster than it travels through air. The sounds made by whales when they communicate with each other can travel for hundreds of miles through the ocean. In theory, the sound of a pistol shot deep underwater could be detected on the other side of the world.

▲ To figure out how far away a thunderstorm is, count the number of seconds between a flash of lightning and the rumble of thunder. Then divide the number of seconds by three and this will give you the distance of the storm in miles. This works because light travels so fast (at 186,000 miles per second) we see the lightning almost immediately. But sound travels a million times more slowly, taking about five seconds to cover one mile.

▲ Many animals have more sensitive hearing than our own (see page 23). Dogs can hear sounds up to 30,000 vibrations per second, cats can hear up to 45,000 vibrations per second and bats can hear up to 160,000 vibrations per second.

▲ Male mosquitoes are attracted to female mosquitoes by the sound of the females' wingbeats.

▲ Many instruments have been played for thousands of years. The ancient Egyptians used a form of harp nearly 5,000 years ago, and the flute was played in Greece in 400 BC.

▲ A piano is a stringed instrument. Its wires are struck by mechanical hammers worked from the keyboard. There may be as many as 88 wires on a modern grand piano.

▲ Some of the longest organ pipes are often 33 feet long.

▲ Some aircraft can fly faster than the speed of sound. As they accelerate through that speed, they send out a shock wave which we can hear. This is called "breaking the sound barrier." The sound is known as a sonic boom and has enough force to shatter windows.

▲ In an old Italian castle near Milan, a fortyfold echo can be heard. Curved walls in the dome of St. Paul's Cathedral, London and in the old Capitol in Washington, D.C. reflect the sound around their curved walls. They are called "whispering galleries" because a whisper at one point on the wall can be heard on the other side of the dome.

▲ Sound waves get weaker as they move out from their starting point. At a distance of 20 feet for example, they are only 25 percent as strong as at 10 feet. And at 39 feet, they are only 6.25 percent as strong.

▲ A humpback whale can make a noise louder than the Concorde on takeoff.

▲ The vibrating vocal chords of a lark rising up into the sky can set in motion 20 tons of air in a sphere of sound waves 3,000 feet in diameter.

GLOSSARY

Acoustics
The study of sound, especially the behavior of sound waves in enclosed spaces, such as concert halls.

Amplify
To make sound louder.

Decibel (dB)
A unit used to measure the loudness of sound. The faintest sound you can hear is about 1 dB, normal conversation is about 60 dB, and a jet aircraft makes sounds of about 120 dB.

Doppler effect
The way a sound changes from a high to a low note if something moves past you very fast. It can be used to measure how fast something is moving.

Echo
A sound which has bounced off something so you hear it again.

Frequency
The number of vibrations in a sound every second. It is measured in Hertz (Hz).

Gas
A substance in which the molecules can move about freely so it has no shape. Air is made up of a mixture of gases.

Hearing aid
A device which makes sounds louder. It may be worn behind the ear, in the ear, on eyeglasses or on the body.

Molecule
The smallest particle of a substance that can exist by itself and still have the properties of that substance.

Pitch
The highness or lowness of a musical note. It depends on the frequency of the vibration causing the sound.

Noise
Unwanted or unpleasant sounds. At about 80 decibels and above, a sound is usually called noise.

Sign language
A communication system consisting of signs made with the hands. The signs stand for words or ideas.

Solid
A substance in which the molecules are held tightly together. A solid has a definite shape.

Sound box
A hollow box with an opening which is placed behind something producing a sound to make the sound louder.

Sound wave
The way in which sound travels with a regular pattern of changes in the pressure of the air.

Supersonic aircraft
Aircraft that can fly faster than the speed of sound.

Vocal cords
The flaps of elastic tissue in your throat which produce sounds as air from the lungs is pushed over them, making them vibrate.

INDEX

Additional photographs:
Chris Fairclough 25 (b);
Hutchison Library 4;
Maggie Murray/Format 25 (t);
Stephen Dalton/NHPA 13 (t);
Martin Wendler/NHPA 23 (t),
Antony Bannister/NHPA 24 (b);
Zefa 9 (t), 12 (b).
Picture Researcher:
Ambreen Husain